SAINT PHILOMENA

The Girl With the Flower Crown

ST SHENOUDA PRESS
8419 Putty Rd,
Putty, NSW, 2330
Sydney, Australia

www.stshenoudapress.com

ISBN 13: 978-1-7638415-8-1

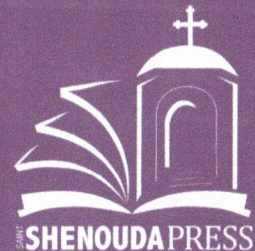

SHENOUDA PRESS

In a palace in Greece,
Lived a beautiful little
girl,
A PRINCESS NAMED
PHILOMENA,
With bouncy brown
curls.

She loved Jesus so much,
And dedicated her life
to Him,
Promising Him she would
do her best,
To remain pure from sin.

As Philomena grew
older,
And her bouncy curls
got longer,
Jesus filled her heart
and mind,
AND HER LOVE FOR HIM
GREW STRONGER.

Lived a mean, unforgiving king. He wanted to start war with her father, and wanted to be ruler of everything.

Hoping to make peace with the king, Philomena's father journeyed far and wide, but the king wouldn't relent, unless Philomena agreed to be his bride.

Philomena's heart belonged only to God, and her refusal filled the king with anger. so he ordered her first punishment, to be thrown into the ocean tied to an anchor.

He was sure she would
drown,
BUT GOD HAD OTHER
PLANS,
He sent two of His
angels,
To bring her out and
loosen her hands.

Again, he tried to hurt Philomena, striking her with a palm until she was sore. But again, the Angels came to her aid, quickly healing her as they did before.

He then shot arrows at Philomena,
But not a single arrow touched her skin, and all of his army that stood watching, began to believe in God as the true King.

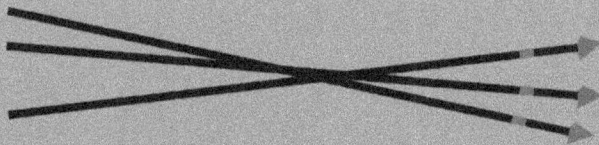

The anger in the king's heart grew, and his pride made him hot with rage, so, he swiftly killed young Philomena, and a GLORIOUS, PURE MARTYR SHE BECAME.

The young princess with the flower crown, arrived in God's embrace, excited and relieved, holding her anchor, palm and arrows, for through the tortures, SHE ALWAYS BELIEVED.

No matter what fears stand in your way, REMEMBER TO KEEP YOUR EYES FIXED ON JESUS' THRONE. He will fill your heart with His peace, and one day will also welcome you home!

GLORY BE TO GOD
FOREVER

AMEN